Prayers With *Love*

Prayers With Love

LUCY TREDWAY

iUniverse, Inc.
Bloomington

PRAYERS WITH LOVE

iUniverse books may be ordered through booksellers or by contacting:

iUniverse
1663 Liberty Drive
Bloomington, IN 47403
www.iuniverse.com
1-800-Authors (1-800-288-4677)

Because of the dynamic nature of the Internet, any web addresses or links contained in this book may have changed since publication and may no longer be valid. The views expressed in this work are solely those of the author and do not necessarily reflect the views of the publisher, and the publisher hereby disclaims any responsibility for them.

Any people depicted in stock imagery provided by Thinkstock are models, and such images are being used for illustrative purposes only.
Certain stock imagery © Thinkstock.

ISBN: 978-1-4620-7002-2 (sc)
ISBN: 978-1-4620-7003-9 (ebk)

Printed in the United States of America

iUniverse rev. date: 11/29/2011

Table of Contents

Dedication

I would like to dedicate these Prayers of Love to:

My deceased mother Luz Maria Cardenas, for planting the seed of love and faith in me, and for teaching me about the greatness of God and for raising me Catholic.

Father Tim Gerickei. For his encouragement, his patience, and his wonderful explanations about the Love of God for us.

Mother Julie of Saint Elizabeth's for all her wisdom and kindness.

My beloved Sacred Heart of Jesus Prayer Group, to whom I owe many thanks for their support and kindness to me as well as their great faith, kindness and love for God. May our Lord bless everyone of them always!

Very importantly, I also dedicate this work to my dear husband, Dennis L. and my children—Dennis A. and Billy—each of whom I love very much.

Introduction

After many years of struggle trying to understand what it was that
God wanted me to do with my life, I came to the realization that we
are all given different gifts and that God will lead us to do
His Will if we place our total trust in Him.

I have always prayed all the regular prayers that I was taught while
growing up, and I read many booklets that contained wonderful
writings from other people. These were all sufficient at the time and
fulfilled my need for prayer. As my spirit grew with love for God so
was the need for other kinds of prayer. And not knowing where to find
it I began to talk to God, just to talk to Him, and pour out my love for
Him as if He was standing right in front of me. As a result, my love
for Him grew stronger and stronger, and my need to tell Him how I
felt grew as well.
In the last fey years, I decided to put in writing my prayers and to
share with others the great gift of love I have received

Every prayer is a testament of love, and humility. I hope that you,
dear reader, are inspired by them and feel the same love that I felt,
when I wrote these "Prayers With Love" will help you to attain eternal
salvation—by dying sincerely repentant and, therefore, in the State
of Grace. Be mindful at all times that: "For many are called, but few
chosen." (Matt. 20:16, 22:14). (Douay-
Rheims, the true Holy Bible.)

An Offering In Faith

Come Holy Spirit, enlighten my soul. Show me the way to understand the writings before me. O Lord, guide, protect and enable me that I may continually remain in a State of Grace all the days of my life to fulfill Your wishes and to be able to accept. Your Divine Will. Please do hear my prayers, Dear Lord, and please strengthen me so that I will always accept Your Will. Grant me that by meditating on these writings, I may grow in holiness and glorify the Trinity this day and each day for he rest of my life on earth . . . and for all eternity! Open my eyes so that I will always see You in others and glorify You all the more by helping them, being mindful that whatsoever we do for them we actually do for You. Grant that I may see You in others and be a fruitful servant for Your glory and honor. Amen.

Thoughts

1. Ask God for strength, faith and courage and He will guide you in every endeavor.
2. Nature is a gift from God. He gave it to us to enjoy in all its magnificent beauty.
3. Let us protect the earth and take good care of it before it is too late.
4. To love God is to love our neighbor: black, white, brown, poor, rich, good, or bad. Let God be the judge of our neighbor's actions. Do not try to do His job for Him; He does not need our help. He is God!
5. We do not need someone to tell us when we do right or wrong. God has given us the most accurate tool as the ultimate instrument of self-assessment. It is called "our conscience."
6. The birds in the sky do not hesitate to fly from tree to tree or to care for their young. God provides for their needs. Why is it that we hesitate every day of our lives worrying about all the things that we may need? Where is our faith? Are we not more precious to God than the birds?
7. Do a good deed every day, and feel the rewards in everything you do.
8. Praise God every day and thank Him for your life. He is your Creator!
9. The happiness that you feel in your heart is a gift from God: it is not something that you earned.

My Eternal Salvation

Lord! Nourish my soul with your bread of life and purify me with your Precious Blood.

I want to join in the sufferings of your Sorrowful Passion and die for your love.

If I could only see your face to tell you how much I love you?

Oh Lord! Let my heart feel your love. Help my soul understand the sorrows of your Mother's Immaculate Heart.

I want to follow you in Calvary. Let me prostrate my wretched body before your Majesty, and tell you how ardently I adore you. In you I trust. In you I believe.

I want to be consumed by the fire of your divinity, and I want to surrender to your Omnipotent Love.

Lord, my soul yearns for you! I love you so much. And yet I don't love you enough.

Show me the way to my cross, and show me how to rejoice in my sufferings so I can unite myself to your Sorrowful Salvation.

My Lord! Rescue me from my iniquities. Come! Don't delay.

My soul thirsts for you. My heart yearns for your love.

I keep searching for you in the darkness of my life. Come Jesus my love! Light up the way to my salvation and to my redemption. Amen.

An Offering of Love
(Bouquet of Flowers for My Lord)

Lord help me appreciate my sufferings as blessings that You have
bestowed upon me
When I am in pain, let me shed tears of joy knowing that You are by
my side at all times
If I ever feel overwhelmed by my burdens, let me prostrate myself
before Your divinity, and ask
You for strength, guidance, and patience
Help me see You in all the little things just like St.
Therese did.
Help me, that I may offer myself to You as a living sacrifice for Your
Infinite glory and for
Your everlasting love
Let my actions and my thoughts be an everlasting offer to You.
Receive them Oh Lord! As a bouquet of flowers that I can send to you
as an offering of great love.

Warm Waters From Heaven'

My Lord, Your love is like soft, warm water from Your ocean of divine mercy that bathes my soul and inspires my life to follow You and want to do Your
Will.
O Merciful God, clothe me with Your divine rays and fill my sinful being with the desire to love You with all my heart.
You are the only reason for my existence. You are the
Master of my creation and You are the center of my life. Protect me, I plea! Help me to recognize my faults and to be repentant of them. I only want to fulfill my mission in this, our broken world.
O Lord, My love, fill me with Your precious Blood and guide me to my eternal home!
I am anxiously waiting to be with You. I will work every day of my life to serve You until the day that I can see Your divine face in Heaven.
I give You my heart, my spirit, and my soul. Mold me to be what You want me to be. I will forever love
You, for You are my Lord! Amen

My Saviour

Lord, I am in the trenches of an evil war fighting for my Soul. I call
Your name and I reach out to You for protection. I recall Your words
filled with love and Your promises to save me from my enemies. O
Lord, where are You?

Why can I not see Your face? My sins have covered me with filth and
I know that I am not worthy of
Your mercy or Your protection.

Please, I beg of You, have pity on this wretched sinner.

Come, My Lord, I plea. Cover me with Your
Precious Blood and grant me salvation.

Send Your angels to guide me away from the shadows of impurity and
sin. I will not succumb to the evils of this world. I will continue to
fight all the rest of my days knowing that You are with me.

Take me, Lord, I am Yours. Evil has no power over me. You are the
Master of my life,. I surrender to
Your divinity and I claim You as my Lord. Amen.

Jesus, My Saviour'

Jesus, My Saviour,
I belong to You!
Jesus, source of my longing,
I belong to You!
Jesus, Master of all Creation,
I belong to You!
Jesus, Treasure Divine,
I belong to You!
Jesus, cover me with Your Precious Blood,
I belong to You!
Jesus, You are my strength,
I belong to You!
Jesus, hide me in Your Precious Wounds,
I belong to You!
Jesus, my great love,
I belong to You!
Jesus, You wipe my tears and You give me comfort,
I belong to You!
Jesus, for Whom there is nothing impossible,
I belong to You!
Jesus, Protector of Life,
I belong to You!
Jesus, Son of the Eternal Father,
I belong to You!
Jesus, my light in the darkness,
I belong to You
Jesus, I trust in You
I surrender my body, my soul and my spirit to You.
From this day on, I promise to serve You.
I submit myself to Your divine will.
Come Holy Spirit and give me the graces I need to
Live my life for Your glory and honor. Amen

Lord Save Me

O Lord, save me from the fires of Hell and protect me from my foes.
The enemy lurks in the darkness and conspires to take my soul.
Save me, O Jesus, cover me with Your Precious Blood.
Pierce my heart with an arrow aflame with Your divinity!
I will fear no evil and I will not fear death, for Your mercy sustains my soul.
I will face my enemies with Your strength and I will face death
covered with Your Precious Blood.
Nothing can harm me. I belong to You, my God!
I will stand strong throughout my trials and I will believe in your
promises.
Lord, sanctify my soul and show me Your great mercy.
I am a sinner, full of repentance, and I am a servant of
Your divine love.
Protect Your servant, O Lord, I depend on You for my salvation. Have
pity on me!
Rescue me! I trust in You! Amen.

Thanksgiving
Jesus, My Lord

When I feel sad, give me comfort.
When I feel lonely, put Your arms around me.
When I feel despair, let me know that You are by my side listening to my cry.
When I think that the world has abandoned me, let me know that You will never leave me.
When I feel empty, fill me with Your Precious Blood.
When I think that I am in control for my own life, enlighten me so I know that I am nothing without You.
When I feel happy, let me know that joy comes from You
When I go to bed a night, let me thank You for another day filled with Your love and mercy.
When I go about my chores, let me use my works for Your glory and honor.
When I feel pain, let me offer it to You for the conversion of sinners and Your great love.
When I am near death, let me praise You and thank You for my life, one more time.
Look at me with pity, O Lord, when I finally enter into Your Kingdom, and have mercy on my soul.
When you speak Your divine words of justice, let me prostrate myself before Your Great Majesty and adore You.
I am Your servant, My Lord. You have given me a life full of blessings and love. I will praise You forever. Amen.

A Prayer of Love and Hope

Let the divine mercy and love of Our Lord Jesus guide us into
holiness by the Precious Blood that He shed for us. Let His divine
heart take us into His abode and hide us from the evils of this world.
May the love and protection of our Blessed Mother guide us with
her infinite love for her Most Beloved Son, Our Lord, Jesus. May the
Holy Spirit teach us and enlighten us in the ways of suffering and
sacrifice for the love of Our Saviour and for His glory and honor.
May God grant us the forbearance and continuance to follow Him in
the Way of the Cross, that we may be able to rejoice in our sufferings
and some day rejoice with the angels before His Great Majesty.
Amen.

My Answer to You, Lord

You asked me, Lord: "Where do I place You in my day?"
I will humbly answer, You are my day and You are my night;
You are my sadness and You are my joy;
You are my failures and You are my success;
You are the air that I breathe and You are the thoughts that I think;
You are my future and You are my past;
You are my hope and in You I trust.
In short, My Lord, I will humbly say to answer the question that You
asked me: "Where do I place You in my day?"
My Lord, I will always place You in my heart each day;
You are not just part of my daily life . . .
Oh no, My Lord, You are my life!

A Prayer of Forbearance

At the twilight of the day, I reflect upon my works, and
I try to consider all I have ever done.
The scale of my life keeps an even balance, and the conflict grows
larger within my soul.
I remind myself of the importance of fairness knowing that Almighty
God is so merciful and just.
I quietly sit down and gather my thoughts, remembering my own
sorrows, and remembering my faults.
With a peaceful resolution I recount my long, long journey, knowing
that my efforts and my hardships will determine where I go.
I will endure, I will trust and I will know that there is hope. I will
claim a life of blessings, and I will give thanks to my Saviour, Lord.
I will try to be more humble, and I will pray, and pray some more. I
will beg my Lord for mercy, and I will always praise His love.
His benevolence will guide me to the very end of time.

Prayer of Faith

Lord, increase my faith in You, more and more every day.
Help me to increase my trust in You.
Let me see Your radiance in the poor and in the hungry.
Pierce the depths of my soul with the rays of Your
Sacred Heart.
I want to feel Your love in the midst of my sorrows.
I want to feel the sorrow of Your passion in the midst of my love for You.
Chain my heart to Your heart.
I am a slave to Your love.
Let my redemption be the light that will guide me to
Your throne.
I can only hope to be in the shadow of Your mercy.
Let me stay inside of Your compassionate heart as the servant that I am.
Let this be my prayer for the Glory of God. Amen.

A Prayer of Hope

Mother of God, you are the vessel of hope that will carry me to your Divine Son, Our Lord, Jesus Christ.

You are the bridge between Heaven and earth.

I know that through your loving and merciful intercession, Our Lord will have mercy on me and I will remain faithful to Him.

I know that you will guide me and protect me as a mother protects her children until the day that I can see the face of my Beloved Lord, your Son, Jesus.

O Mother of God, my Mother, keep me safe, hold me in your arms.

Protect me from anything that may interfere with my salvation and my love for God.

From now on, I will consecrate myself to my Lord Jesus, to His Sacred Heart and to you, Mary, to your Immaculate Heart.

O Mary, Most Blessed Mother of God, intercede for me. You are my Mother, in you I trust. Amen.

A Prayer of Love

Lord your love is greater than the depth of the sea
Greater than the warmth of the sun
Greater than the might of the thunder
Your Mercy is softer than the rain in the spring
Gentler than the lamb in the meadow
And kinder than a mother's heart
Your benevolence embraces us when we need it the most. You bring
comfort to our broken hearts, and You appease our troubled minds.
You rejoice when we come to You, and reassure us of Your endless
love and Your protection.
O My Lord, keep me, protect me, and guide me to
You. I am helpless without you!
You are my shield, and You are my strength! Let
Your infinite love be my salvation.

A Prayer of Service

Lord, move my heart, that I can see You in my brother. Blind my eyes
that I do not see his faults.

Show me how to feel his sorrows, and the willingness to respond to all.
Give me the wisdom to understand Your orders, and the compassion to
fulfill your goals.

Help me to trust in Your great divinity.

Come, enter my heart with Your deepest Love!

Help me to be transformed from a wretched creature into a loving and
caring soul, that I can serve others from now and forever, until I see You in
Your Majestic Hall. Amen.

A Prayer of Thanksgiving

Lord, I can feel Your protection on me like a divine shield.
I can rest now. I fear no evil. My trust is in You, Lord.
No Malice has power over me. I can feel Your love.
You guide me through the tempestuous roads of my life, and You hold
my hand so I will not stumble.
Your divine guide shows me the way, and I can see
Your radiance in the light.
Your Almighty hand has reached into my soul, and
You have granted me a place in Your omnipotent kingdom.
O My Lord, how great You are! I will praise Your name forever, and I
will thank You until the day I die. Amen

A Prayer of Trust

My Lord, I know You! I trust in Your merciful love and
Your protection.
During the day when I feel the burden of my troubled life,
Lord, hide me in Your Precious Wounds.
When I am restless and cannot sleep because of my uncertainties and
fears; Lord, cover me with Your
Precious Blood.
When I feel that my cross is too heavy to carry and I cannot go on;
Lord, let me remember Your divine passion and all the pain You
suffered for me.
When I think I can do everything for myself and I forget that You are
my creator; Lord, come and gently guide me back on the right path to
my salvation.
When I forget that I am here to serve You and to love my brother;
Lord, let me feel the humility I need to do Your works.
When I forget to thank You and to praise You for the blessings You
have bestowed upon me; Lord, grant me the wisdom to remember that
without You nothing is possible.
When I finally entrust my soul to You in the last moments of my life;
Lord, remember that I tried to do the best that I could to serve You.
Now I have nothing to fear because I believe in Your promises and I
trust in Your Love.

A Soldier of Love

Lord, I am a soldier in the army of Your love. I am filled with Your
Spirit. I seek Your wisdom to fulfill my task.
Give me Your orders! I am ready to serve. Give me the challenge that
You chose for me.
My arms are ready for battle. My spirit is filled with joy.
I have all I need to conquer—my faith, Your strength, and
Your love.
Give my Your orders, I am ready for battle! In your name I will
conquer; for Your glory and for Your love! Amen.

A Total Surrender

My Lord and My God., I know that You are alive in the
Blessed Sacrament of the altar.
I can see You with my heart and I can hear You in my soul.
Come to me, My Lord, I am Yours.
I never want to be apart from You.
I give You my life, my soul, and everything that I am.
I empty my heart to You. Take it. Fill it with Your love and Your
Precious Blood.
Take it and fill it with Your own heart, so it is no longer my heart, but
Your heart.
Shape me, mold me, and use me in any way that You want.
I only want to love You and to serve You.
I would rather not exist, than to be without Your love and
Your protection.
I adore You in the most Blessed Sacrament!
O My Lord, do not ever let me be apart from You!
You are my life and my salvation.
I will forever love You, I am Yours. Amen

Praise to God

My Lord, I want to contemplate Your divine mercy every hour of the day.
I want to exalt Your majesty forever.
I want to praise Your graces endlessly.
Let my heart be immersed in the pool of Your divine benevolence.
Let Your divine rays permeate my own soul.
O Divine Master, guide me through the road of salvation!
Let my heart succumb to Your divinity once and for all!
I rebuke anything that is against You, for You are the greatest! You are my all!

Prayer of Gratitude for Life

My Lord, Your penetrating gaze pierces my being until it reaches my soul.
My heart shivers with emotion at the thought of Your merciful love.
The knowledge of being made in the image of my God, is more than
my poor human nature can measure or understand!
I am unique and I am so special because I resemble what
You are.
I thank You for my creation, for this lovely piece of art!
The meaning of Your creation is unutterably great.
Thank You for my existence; I want to thank You for my life!
Thank You God, thank You Father, thank You Son, thank
You Holy Ghost, that I am a child of Your everlasting light!

Holy Trinity Divine Love

Come Divine Father, Omnipotent Love, Sculptor of Bodies and
Master of Hearts; You created me in the image of
Your Beloved Son.
How can I ever thank You for such a magnificent grant?
Come almighty Jesus, Son of the Living God, and fill my heart with
compassion, with humility and with love.
Come Holy Spirit, Enlightener of Souls, come and let it be my quest
just to love You above all.
Holy Trinity, please come set my whole being ablaze!
Let me surrender my existence to Your divine love.
Let me praise You with Your angels, let me thank You with my heart,
that I will forever be grateful for Your mercy and Your love.

Jesus, My Love

I woke up this morning, thinking of You.
I wish I could tell You how I feel inside.
I wish I could say what is in my heart.
I see You in the flowers, I see You in the rain.
I see You in the chores that I do every day.
I see You in my laughter, I see You in my pain.
Just thinking of You brings tears to my eyes.
I yearn for Your loving, I love You so much.
I want to be with You, My Jesus, My Love.

Prayer to My Guardian Angel

Angel of the Lord, my guardian, my protector, my companion, and my friend; walk with me today, remain close, catch me if I fall.
There are so many trials in my life. Hold me steady. Do not let me be apart from you.
God has sent you to guide me. Please hold me and hide me under your wings. Show me the way. I want to follow my Lord in the Way of the Cross.
My guardian Angel, my friend, keep me safe today.
I only want to do my best to do the Lord's Will

A Total Surrender

My Lord and My God., I know that You are alive in the
Blessed Sacrament of the altar.
I can see You with my heart and I can hear You in my soul.
Come to me, My Lord, I am Yours.
I never want to be apart from You.
I give You my life, my soul, and everything that I am.
I empty my heart to You. Take it. Fill it with Your love and Your
Precious Blood.
Take it and fill it with Your own heart, so it is no longer my heart, but
Your heart.
Shape me, mold me, and use me in any way that You want.
I only want to love You and to serve You.
I would rather not exist, than to be without Your love and
Your protection.
I adore You in the most Blessed Sacrament!
O My Lord, do not ever let me be apart from You!
You are my life and my salvation.
I will forever love You, I am Yours. Amen

My Love For You Lord

My Lord, You have shown me the treasure of Your divine heart. You
penetrated the depths of my own insignificant heart with Yours.
I know that I can find refuge in You, when I am in despair.
O My Lord, I seek shelter in Your divine wounds!
When I see Your divine face, my heart melts with gratitude and
love. I do not dare to raise my eyes up to You, for I am not worthy of
anything that comes from such divinity.
How can I show You my love? How can I ever do Your
Will? I am so insignificant, and I am such a sinner. You are so good Lord!
I cannot express my love for You. I am just a miserable human being!
My love is from my heart, and not from my lips.
I can only tell You in my own humble way, that You are everything to me,
that I want nothing else unless it comes from You, and that I love no other!
You are my love and my salvation. I will always thank
You for creating me. I love You. Amen.

Prayer for Forgiveness

Lord, I have sinned! I know that I have hurt You. Please forgive me!
Let my heart bleed with sorrow for all the pain that I have caused You.
Let me cry a million tears in repentance for my sins!
Lord, hear my plea! I am sorry for my sins!
Receive me back into Your flock. I am Your lost sheep, but I want to
come home. Please forgive me!
Hide me in Your Precious Wounds. Grand me Your protection. I am
seeking refuge in You.
I want to remain faithful, knowing that Your unwavering love will be
my salvation.

A Prayer of Hope

Mother of God, you are the vessel of hope that will carry me to your
Divine Son, Our Lord, Jesus
Christ.
You are the bridge between Heaven and earth.
I know that through your loving and merciful intercession, Our Lord
will have mercy on me and I will remain faithful to Him.
I know that you will guide me and protect me as a mother protects her
children until the day that I can see the face of my Beloved Lord, your Son,
Jesus.
O Mother of God, my Mother, keep me safe, hold me in your arms.
Protect me from anything that may interfere with my salvation and my
love for God.
From now on, I will consecrate myself to my Lord
Jesus, to His Sacred Heart and to you, Mary, to your Immaculate Heart.
O Mary, Most Blessed Mother of God, intercede for me. You are my
Mother, in you I trust. Amen.

To Love Our Blessed Mother Is To Love Jesus

O Mary, the Immaculate Conception, the true example of all virtues,
O Mother of God, never let me part from you—
You, who suffered the seven greatest sorrows, give me the strength
and fortitude in my own sorrows.
You who knows what it is like to be a wife and mother guide me, dear
Mother, so I can serve God through fulfilling the obligations of my life.
You who are the example of all virtues, help me to live a virtuous life
through our Lord Jesus.
You, who became the greatest example of patience, help me to be
patient, and always to have a kind word for everyone I meet.
You who obediently agreed to become the mother of our living God,
help me to be obedient to the Ten
Commandments, and thus to follow Our Lord.
You, who have showed us your Immaculate Heart, help me always to
consecrate my children, and myself, to Your
Immaculate Heart, that is a fountain of mercy and love.
O Mother of God, My Mother, help me to learn how to love, so I can
love God above everything and follow you, Dear Mother, so I can live
in the shadow of your perfect love,
Through Jesus Our Lord. Amen.

Saint Therese, Little Flower

Saint Therese, teach me how to embrace my sufferings and offer them to Our Lord, just like you did.

Teach me how to look for the good in the people I meet and to see Jesus in them, just like you did.

Teach me how to give myself to Our Lord and to offer to Him everything I do, just like you did.

Teach me how to trust in His merciful love with blind faith, just like you did.

Teach me how to pray from the bottom of my heart and to remain faithful to Him, just like you did.

O Little Flower, help me to follow Our Lord in your steps, to be humble at heart and to live totally for Him, to have unshakable faith, just like you did.

I trust Little Flower that you will pray for me, that I can be little, and grow in love for Him, just like you did!

Amen

His Divine Artistry

My Lord, I saw You this morning in the rays of the sun!
I heard You last night in the roar of the thunder.
I felt Your embrace when the wind stroked my face.
I noticed Your touch with the first drops of rain.
I marveled in awe at the colors of Your rainbow, as I sat and wondered
at the beauty of it all.
I love You so much, that my words cannot define, what I am feeling
inside when I witness Your might.
Remain with me Lord, and overlook my weaknesses!
I know that I have sinned and I hurt You many times.
Yet I know that You still love me. You show me every day that Your
mercy and love is greater than any of my mistakes.
I saw Your kindness shining through all Your marvelous deeds, so
please my Lord, forgive me for all my errors! I plea!
Send down again Your sunshine, Your wind, Your thunder and Your rain.
Let me see the colors of Your rainbow once again.
I need to see Your brilliance and I need to feel Your love.
Come, Lord of Might and Power. Come, Lord, O Great
Divine!
Let me see the splender of Your Glory one more time.

Thank You God!

Today I start a new day full of confidence and hope.
I know that God is within me. I feel His presence.
My faith keeps growing each day. My struggles remain the same; but
knowing that He is with me will help me in carrying the cross.
He never departs from me. I know He promised me that!
His gentle and loving way will guide me straight towards the light.
I am anxious to get to Heaven, and see the glory of my
God, because of His mercy and love.
He will allow me to enter, and then I can thank Him again for all of
His mercy and for all of His Love.

A Prayer of Submission

Lord, You have shown me how much You love me.
My weaknesses are so great!
Help me understand Your love so that I can truly trust in
You.
Let Your might overshadow my insignificant humanity so that I can
accept that I truly depend on You.
Let not my arrogance and pride destroy what You have created.
Let not my invalid sense of perfection determine the path that You
chose for me.
I want to submit to Your everlasting grandeur and accept
Your Will for me.
I want to humbly prostrate myself before You so as to tell
You how much I love You and beg You to have mercy on me. Amen.

Searching My Heart For God

I looked for You last night, as I was laying in bed.
I searched my mind for You, and my heart ached in despair.
I looked in the light far away, when I thought that Your were hiding.
And I tried and tried so hard, but everything I did was in vain.
Where were You?
Why didn't you come?
I waited so long for You.
I spent the night searching, in my thoughts and in my dreams.
Tonight I will try again,
I will look for You some more.
I will search deep in my heart, and I will call Your name again.
If You hear a voice, please come,
It is my heart calling for You.
I am searching for just a glance, of Your sweetness and Your love.
I miss You. Please come.

LORD

I see You in every flower.
I see You in every bird.
I see You after the rain, when the sky is so blue.
When I wake up in the morning and when I go to bed at night, I see
Your might in the light and I hear
Your omnipotence in the thunder.
Your love is in the wind and in the softness of the rain.
O My Lord and My God, let me praise You!
Let my lips call Your name.
Jesus! Jesus! Jesus!!!
I surrender to Your mercy and I surrender to Your
Love.
I am Yours! I only want to do Your Will. I want to love You more and
more. Do not ever let me part from You!
I am nothing without You! I will always praise Your name forever and
ever. I love You! Amen.

A Proclamation of Love

There is nothing more infinite than the love of God.
I will fear nothing for His protection is great!
He hides me in His heart where His love is more solid than a majestic rock.
There is nothing more pure and unwavering than His great compassion.
He relieves the sorrows that distress my soul, and He brings deliverance to my troubled heart,
Oh how great You are, My God!
I will ask the angels to join me in praise, and I will glorify forever Your name.
Give me Your love, I humbly ask; that I can trust in You, O Lord, to acclaim Your glory and proclaim Your love!

Prayer for Strength

Lord, give me the faith, the strength, and the courage to change the way I am.
Grant me the wisdom to see my own faults.
Help me to rectify my weaknesses.
Give me the courage to love my enemies, and the patience to help my friends.
Save me from the evils of pride and arrogance.
Help me to become humble, patient and charitable.
Give me the graces I need to live a holy life.
I only want to live for You, work for You and die for You.
You are my God, My Lord, and My Saviour.
My heart belongs to You.
I love no other. Jesus, save me, I am Yours.

Praises to God

You stayed with me, when I was in pain.
You wiped my tears, when sorrow came.
You gave me the strength to carry my cross.
You loved me! I know You helped me through it all.
I want to thank You and praise Your name.
O Jesus My Love, please keep me in Your heart!
Cover me, I beg You, with Your Precious Blood.
And lead me, I plea, on this final hour, back to Your abode of
compassionate love, that I may praise
Your glory and honor, and bless Your name forever. Amen.

Plea to Repent

Blessed be the Triune God forever and ever. His omnipotent love is great.
His mercy is unlike anything else
His love shines like the brightest star in the firmament.
His might holds together our insignificant humanity.
Thank You, Lord, for all that You do for us.
We do not deserve anything that comes from You.
We thank You for the patience that You have with us miserable and
ungrateful people.
O My Lord, sinners that we are, give us another chance, I implore You!
Let Your Spirit come upon us, so we can repent and turn away from sin.
Let us repent from all the pain that we have caused to one another.
And especially let us repent from all the pain that we have caused to You.
O My Lord and My God, have mercy on us
We deserve Nothing from You. Please have pity!
Amen.

Prayer for Our Holy Father

Lord bestow all your graces and Your blessings on
Our Holy Father so He can truly guide us in union with Your Divine
Spirit on the road of salvation through the teachings of our beloved
Holy Roman
Catholic Church so that together with all Your angels and Saints we
may glorify You forever and ever.
Protect Him, Lord, from the obscurities of this world and cover Him
with Your Precious Blood. We ask this in the name of Our Lord, Jesus
Christ.b